The Official Guide To Office Wellness

101 Techniques for the Office or Cubicle

William R. Vitanyi, Jr.

Bayla Publishing
Edinboro, Pennsylvania
USA

Bayla Publishing
12820 Kline Road
Edinboro, Pa. 16412

www.baylapublishing.com

First Edition

Cover designed by Dorota Swies
www.LyonsDenProductions.net

Library of Congress Control Number: 2006905310

ISBN: 0-978-5600-2-7
ISBN 13: 978-0-978-5600-2-7

Printed in the United States of America

Also by William R. Vitanyi, Jr.

Kyuboria
learn to think inside the box

Clint Palmer is a man with a mission. For years he has toiled in the obscurity of his cubicle, an obedient State Worker mindlessly following the rules. But now he wants out, and when a grant becomes available that could fund his dream company, Clint is ecstatic.

But there's a catch. To qualify for the grant, Clint must get fired. But there's a catch. The State never fires anyone.

This is the pathetically humorous tale of one man's escalating schemes to get fired from an organization that doesn't know how. If you work in a cubicle and dream of escape, you must read this book. You'll never look at four walls the same again. It's cubicle humor with a twist.

Palm Sunday
they know what you're saying…

Everyone uses the Internet. Email, file transfers, online transactions, browsing…

And now it's being used to take profiling to the next level. A secret private agency is monitoring Internet communications on a massive scale to create a 'societal profile', invading the privacy of millions of unsuspecting Internet users.

But it's for your own good…

When a stolen PDA opens a window into the clandestine activities of the all-seeing agency, all bets are off. Suspense abounds in this high tech tale of intrigue and betrayal.

These books available through most online book vendors, or ask for them at your favorite bookstore.

For more information visit www.baylapublishing.com

The Official Guide To Office Wellness

William R. Vitanyi, Jr.

Bayla Publishing Edinboro, Pennsylvania USA

In Grateful Acknowledgement

This book would not have been possible without the generous participation of one hundred volunteer models from Edinboro University of Pennsylvania and the surrounding community. They gave of their time and posed in the most outrageous positions in offices and cubicles simply because they were asked. Thank you, each of you, for your indispensable help with this project.

The following individuals provided proofreading and editing services with great professionalism and skill:

Marilyn Goellner
Jan Walker

To those who encouraged me: you are priceless. Thank you!

The Official Guide To Office Wellness

WARNING

This book is a spoof.

Do no actually use this book as part of any exercise program, real or imagined.

The models used here are professionals, but not as models or in any capacity related to any program of health or exercise that could by any stretch of the imagination actually benefit anyone in any way.

Do not emulate what is being done in these pictures. If you do, and you get hurt, it's your own fault. So don't.

Bayla Publishing is not responsible for use of this book in any capacity except as humorous amusement. Return this book at once if you are entertaining any thoughts at all of using it for self improvement, for you have made a terrible mistake. Just put it back on the shelf and slowly walk away.

For an actual workout, try skipping.

This has been a disclaimer.

Using this Manual

The design of this book is consistent with industry standards regarding cubicle exercise. At the top of each page you will find three lines of text. The first line lists the office malady addressed by the technique. The second line lists the name of the technique, and the third line shows the Latin name of the animal inspiring the technique. The three lines of text, known as a triplet, are followed by a photograph of a model demonstrating the technique.

For best results, mentally perform the pictured technique while two or three coworkers observe. This is known as cubicle imprinting, but can be performed in any office area.

Next, read the text below the photograph. After meditating carefully, perform the technique to the best of your ability. If you have not cleared this with a qualified physician, skip this step and simply continue to visualize.

Most important—enjoy. For without joy we have wasted the wisdom of the animals.

Leadership Occlusion
Rough-Skinned Newt Lunge Stance
Status taricha granulose

To motivate others in the office environment you must exude poise and confidence, but effective leadership also requires practice. The Rough-Skinned Newt Lunge Stance provides the opportunity to exercise your administrative muscles, and trains you to overcome operational obstacles. Regular use of this stance also enhances supervisory proficiency and may strengthen inspirational capacity. This technique should be practiced three times daily, and is especially effective when used before staff meetings.

Gossip Precision Deficiency
Dogfish Shark Bridge Position
Squalus acanthias

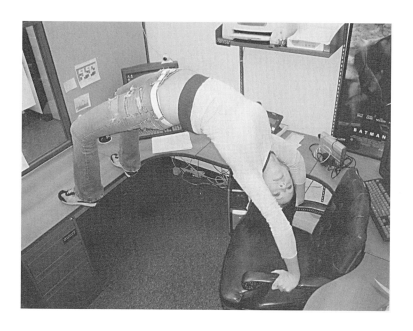

Gossip is the lifeblood of corporate communication, but like any specialized skill it should only be practiced by trained professionals. Without proper instruction, the novice may be inclined to disseminate rumors that lack therapeutic precision. The Dogfish Shark Bridge Position suppresses the body's tendency towards indiscriminate news sharing, and at the same time strengthens gossip fundamentals. This technique is perfect for new employees, or as a refresher for old timers.

Acute Supply Deficiency
Turkey Vulture Weighted Arm Stance
Cathartes aura

In nature there is a phenomenon known as catch-up syndrome, and this tendency to hoard in the aftermath of shortage also occurs in the office supply arena. You will never use five thousand binder clips, so let it go. The Turkey Vulture long ago learned the value of moderation, and we should follow his example. This position of strength and balance improves your ability to endure perennial shortage of office supplies, and also increases bone mass. For counterweight a stapler or unwanted coffee mug works best.

Chewing Sensitivity Disorder
Largemouth Bass Extended Leg Position
Micropterus salmoides

The loud eater is a well-documented office inhabitant. There is perhaps no greater irritant than the repeated crunch of a pretzel, or the crispy smack of a red delicious apple on a brisk autumn afternoon. Sitting in quiet rage is not the answer. While waiting for blessed silence, perform the Largemouth Bass Extended Leg Position. It may not stop the gastronomic madness, but this voracious lake dweller reminds us of the importance of tolerance. Embrace the crunchiness as you ponder the infinite.

There is nothing wrong with sleeping in your cubicle. Sometimes, in fact, the real difficulty is in attaining full REM sleep during work hours. To prepare your brain for synaptic rest, assume the Pacific Herring Grip Ankle Position until drowsiness occurs. This raised leg posture inhibits the formation of zeal, while increasing doze proficiency. The peaceful state induced by this method has been described as hypnotic, so do not perform this technique without first clearing your calendar.

Hyper Enthusiasm
Meadow Slug Swift River Position
Deroceras leave

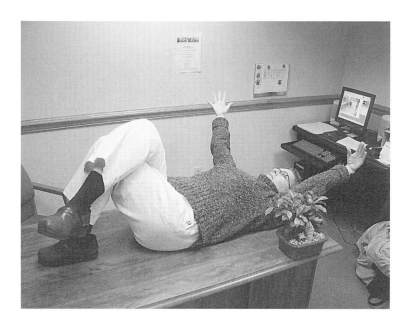

There are times when you want to accomplish something at work, but who has the energy? Well, now you can! Assume the above position ten minutes before any work-related task, and soon you will have as much energy as the Meadow Slug itself. When performing this technique elevate your arms above your head, open your hands wide, and close your eyes. Foliage has been shown to increase efficacy. For best results incorporate with a balanced diet, regular exercise, vitamin supplements, and a good night's sleep.

Office Fugue
Trumpeter Swan Unitary Leg Stance
Cygnus buccinator

In times of stress a worker will sometimes travel to another office or cubicle without any awareness of the journey. This can be a confusing episode for everyone. The Trumpeter Swan Unitary Leg Stance is a centering position that both relieves stress and keeps you in one spot. The key to success is to mimic the majestic wings of the swan with your outstretched arms. The raised foot can briefly touch your leg, but should not fall below the level of the ankle. Center your gaze on the left hand, and hold for three minutes. Repeat.

Workaholism
Clark's Nutcracker Inverted Thumb Stance
Nucifraga columbiana

For you, enough is not enough. Monday morning is too long to wait, so you arrive Sunday evening. Lunch is an opportunity to start a new project. Breaks are for polishing reports. You work too hard, and you know it, but you just can't help yourself. You have Workaholism. Don't panic. The road to recovery begins with elevation. The Clark's Nutcracker Inverted Thumb Stance is an effective high altitude production inhibitor. The perspective provided by this technique will make you wonder why you ever bothered.

Celebratory Imbalance
Brook Stickleback Supine Position
Culaea inconstans

Office parties are great, but they almost always include cake. The result is unusually high sugar levels, and frequent silliness. This unfortunate byproduct can negatively impact career aspirations, so it is important to build up resistance to this potent force. The Brook Stickleback Supine Position is a sugar neutralizer, and enhances natural somberness. Synchronized leg and arm posturing are essential to the success of this position, which may also stimulate enzyme production. Use before and after office celebrations.

Tune Proximity Aversion
Rusty Blackbird Indexed Ear Position
Euphagus carolinus

It is human nature to scorn music chosen by others. Perhaps this is why musical appreciation seldom survives a cubicle wall. Fortunately, the human brain can be trained to filter out unwanted melodies, although it takes rigorous training. Start with the Rusty Blackbird Indexed Ear Position. Beginners should insert the finger no further than the first knuckle, but with practice may eventually achieve second or even third knuckle proficiency. For best results remember to bend the knees, maintain a forward gaze, and concentrate.

Break Amnesia
Arctic Ground Squirrel Clock Arm Position
Spermophilus parryi

Breaks are much more than a legally mandated benefit, yet some workers habitually forget this important office ritual. The result can be dangerous isolation and an information vacuum, imperiling the lives of coworkers. Remember to take breaks! The Arctic Ground Squirrel is no stranger to time management, as this technique clearly demonstrates. Imagine that you have clock hands, and bend your elbows in symbolic representation of the passage of time. Use hourly for best results, but remember to rest periodically.

Compensatory Bloat
Golden Garden Spider Low Palm Stance
Argiope aurantia

Some office workers are generous to a fault. No matter how low their pay is, these bighearted employees will never be satisfied with their paycheck. It is simply too much. To assuage the guilt that accompanies this syndrome, try the Golden Garden Spider Low Palm Stance. Let the imagery of this magnificent arachnid fill your mind, as you reach toward the ground with your open palms to demonstrate how low your pay should be. As your hands approach the floor, hook your desk with your foot for balance. Works best on payday.

Boredom
Boreal Chickadee Inverted Chair Position
Poecile hudsonica

With a brain the size of a walnut, the Boreal Chickadee does little of interest to anyone. Nevertheless, this aptly named bird provides both inspiration and diversion. As you raise your right arm, breathe deeply through your left nostril and suck in a torrent of office air. The arm is symbolic of a fast growing tree, perhaps bamboo. Maintain this position until you feel interest returning, but stop at the first sign of dizziness. You may be able to maintain this posture all day by carefully positioning office equipment nearby.

Ambitionism
Northern Pike Hurdle Position
Esox lucius

Undisciplined energy is a powerful, yet chaotic force. Most offices are blessed with one special individual who would gladly do the work of three people, if only he could harness his own enthusiasm. Sadly, such individuals rarely possess the restraint necessary to control their work urge, and usually produce little more than multidirectional bedlam. The Northern Pike Hurdle Position is an example of exhaustion therapy, and should be offered to the over-enthused worker under the guise of a routine work task. Assign as needed.

Keyboard Sensitivity Disorder
Pileated Woodpecker Sedentary Position
Dryocopus pileatus

The Pileated Woodpecker is renowned for its pecking, much like your neighbor's relentless keyboard clicking. To drive this incessant din from your mind requires studied practice, a steady hand, and patience. When you can no longer bear the racket, clear the edge of your desk and assume a reclining side position. Allow your right hand to dangle just above the floor, and extend your left hand limply towards the ceiling. One foot should delicately touch the desktop. This is a purely defensive position which offers temporary relief.

Telephone Inundation Syndrome
Bluegill Scissor Finger Position
Lepomis macrochirus

An unending stream of phone calls can sap the strength of even the most steadfast office worker. Noted for its quick thinking and determination, the Bluegill is the driving force behind this aggressive technique designed to restore your call passion. Pretend your fingers are a pair of scissors, lift your head, and prepare to cut that annoying phone line. But don't. With the scissors poised for the fatal slice, relish the moment of imagined control. Knowing that you *could* make that pretend cut is empowering.

E-phobia
Black Footed Albatross Tri-Limb Position
Phoebastria nigripes

Electronic communications have greatly increased since the inception of email, but some office workers are fearful to embrace this technology. Estimates indicate that e-phobia accounts for seven per cent of unanswered messages, and this number may be growing. The Black Footed Albatross Tri-Limb position helps ease fear of electronic processes by mimicking the three connectors of a transistor, the primary electronic component of early computers. With regular practice your Outlook should improve greatly.

Office Decoration Anxiety
Olympic Mudminnow Knee Stance
Novumbra hubbsi

Sensitivity to décor is an elemental force. As such, it would be unwise to ignore its influence on your workplace ambience, but it is also unwise to enslave yourself to its demanding perfection. Sometimes this is easier said then done, so at the first sign of Decoration Anxiety, quickly assume the Olympic Mudminnow Knee Stance. From this perspective you will be able to sense even moderate fluctuations in local feng shui. Be persistent, as correct office adornment is an elusive pursuit. Adjust your palm as needed.

File Narcolepsy
Bighorn Sheep Wall Position
Ovus canadensis

Even the best workers are susceptible to the extreme sleepiness induced by repetitive filing. Over time, the chronic fatigue that accompanies File Narcolepsy can have disastrous effects, such as dossier de-sequencing, or file spoilage. Since office workers seldom realize how close they are to complete file failure, it is up to others to be observant. At the first sign of drowsiness, place the affected worker in a restful position, with one foot elevated. It is normal for the arms to reflexively file for several hours.

Promotion Maladaptive Disorder
Magnificent Frigatebird Ascending Heaven Stance
Fregata magnificens

What do you do after you get that big promotion? Sometimes the answer is—panic. If you question why you even applied for the job, then you may be suffering from Promotion Maladaptive Disorder, the inability to adjust to a fantastic new position. Fortunately there is help, in the form of the Magnificent Frigatebird Ascending Heaven Stance. This uplifting technique boosts self confidence and increases personal advocacy. If you don't feel better after five minutes, try a bigger chair.

Activity Report Compilation Disease
Northern Shoveler Rounded Elbow Stance
Anas clypeata

Accountability is a byword of this age. The office is no exception, as managers demand evidence of employee activity in the form of written reports or statements. The conscientious worker will always go the extra mile to produce corporate documentaries that both entertain and inform, but this can be taken to unfortunate extremes. To stop yourself from slipping in that final sarcastic suggestion, assume the Northern Shoveler Rounded Elbow Stance. Hold for two minutes, or until a more productive thought arrives.

Vending Inadequacy
Marine Iguana Inverted Palm Stance
Amblyrhynchus cristatus

It seems so simple for others: select an item, press a button, and remove your treat from the dispenser. Vending is a skill that should be second nature, but for some it is little more than a frustrating obstacle to a full life. Vending disorders are unique in that successful treatment includes both repetitive vending mimicry, and bi-level foot posturing. You may find it helpful as you practice this technique to have a coworker periodically drop a vended item from a distance of about two feet for auditory reinforcement.

Bluescreenism
Wolf Spider Crouching Position
Lycosa aspera

Any computer error is cause for concern, but sometimes things get entirely out of hand. Certain PC based operating systems display a useful blue screen when fatal errors occur, informing the user that meaningful action is no longer possible. However, people need meaning, and without intervention repeated exposure to this phenomenon can be lethal. The Wolf Spider Crouching Position is a binary exercise that replicates a normal computing experience. Periodically switch hands to prevent image burn.

Coworker Adhesion Syndrome
Long Tailed Weasel Stretch Position
Mustela frenata

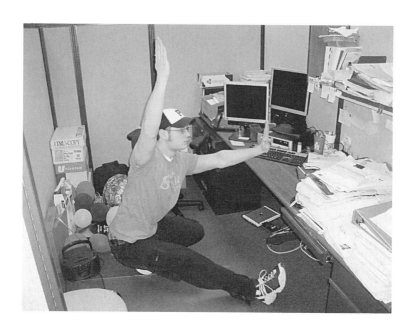

Sometimes a coworker will develop an unusually strong, but unwanted attraction to you. Scientists call this unrequited desire cortical bonding, because of its origin in the primordial cortex, but you just call it a hassle. The difficulty in treating this syndrome lies in communication, which often fails to breech the barrier of love. To ensure a breakthrough, assume a triple redundant posture that both gently rebuffs, and casually threatens. The extended leg is your last line of defense, so be certain it is fully deployed.

Nasal Episode
Spiny Anteater Round Up Position
Tachyglossus aculeatus

Periodically a nearby coworker will disperse a quantity of unfresh air into the atmosphere, severely destabilizing the local ecosystem. Although it is natural to become angry in this situation, such a response only forces you to breathe more deeply. Instead, at the first hint of malodorous intrusion, assume the Spiny Anteater Round Up Position, which safely removes you from the offensive layer of impurity. For additional safety use one arm to promote local air circulation.

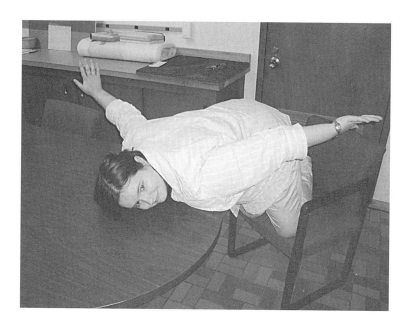

Technology now permits us to learn via webcasts, saving time and travel expense. Unfortunately, many workers zone out just minutes into these electronic gatherings, jeopardizing career aspirations. Don't let this happen to you. To enhance your ability to appear interested in web-based instruction, follow the example of the Horseshoe Crab. With your head placed sideways, extend your arms in a classic display of web-centric enthusiasm. Don't be surprised when others follow your example.

Cooler Phobia
Glass Lizard Bucket Movement
Ophisaurus

When the water cooler is almost empty, you break into an icy sweat. You will do anything to avoid replacing that infernal jug, but you don't know why. You even alter the route you take to your office just so you don't have to walk past your liquid nemesis. It's time to face reality: you have Cooler Phobia. The Glass Lizard Bucket Movement can bring relief, as you slowly acclimate yourself to the act of lifting water. Start with small, half-full pretend buckets, and gradually increase as your tolerance builds. You can do this.

Compliance Disorder
Western Toad Squat Position
Bufo boreas

It's not that you are contrary; you just can't bring yourself to follow the rules. This inability to conform is the primary symptom of Compliance Disorder, one of the higher level submissive ailments common among middle-aged office workers. This condition typically follows years of mindless capitulation, and associated behaviors include bilateral simulated deafness and mutism. The Western Toad Squat Position symbolizes defiant surrender, and helps balance the conflicting demands of work and attitude.

Angst
Grass Pickerel Swimming Desk Position
Psaltriparus minimus

Angst is defined as a feeling of anxiety, apprehension, or insecurity, and is commonly experienced in the office as a result of fighting the inevitable. It is almost always easier to swim with the current, but this does not necessarily yield desired results. If you are going to be a desk rebel, you will frequently encounter strong currents of opposition, and thus, much angst. To successfully battle these eddies of negativity, employ the Grass Pickerel Swimming Desk Position. Correct form is essential, and don't forget to kick.

Input Paralysis
Yellow Perch Raised Peripheral Posture
Perca flavescens

A rare but highly contagious office ailment, Input Paralysis can strike workers of any age or demography. The most notable symptom is a fascination with input devices, but a complete indifference regarding their use. The victim of this nagging condition should be encouraged to rediscover the joy of data entry through exploration and experimentation. Whenever possible, multiple devices should be combined in one session. Some peripheral specialists recommend the use of small plants to ease the process of recovery.

Glaciation Disorder
Emperor Penguin Heel Stance
Salvelinus alpinus

A frigid office environment quickly depletes enthusiasm. While the reason for interpersonal distance can vary, it almost always causes workplace tension. Do not succumb to this pernicious force. Instead, when confronted by a frosty coworker, immediately assume the Emperor Penguin Heel Stance. This noble arctic survivor shows us that even the harshest climate can be endured. In anticipation of potentially icy behavior, wear the colors of the penguin and firmly brace your heels. Foot angle will vary by season.

Chair Retention Disorder
American Bison Surfer Posture
Bos bison

When collecting becomes an obsession, it may be time to seek professional help. When your collection consists of office chairs, more desperate action is called for. The American Bison Surfer Posture is an extreme measure, yet may be the only solution. Forget about the chairs, hop up on the desk, and imagine that you are hanging ten. The rush you will feel is so much more satisfying than gathering chairs, and is also thought to improve cholesterol levels. Hold for two minutes, or until you feel the wave crest.

Messenger Immunity Deficiency
Nile Crocodile Cover Posture
Crocodylus niloticus

Reporting unpleasant corporate news, such as decreased profits or impending layoffs, can be dangerous. There may be little you can do about the facts, but you can certainly limit any personal fallout. The key is to communicate from cover. Assume a position of complete body immersion coupled with unbroken keyboard contact. Be sure your head is shielded by a stout desk. This position strengthens your ability to deliver negative reports without repercussions, and also increases arm flexibility. Best when used late in the day.

Cubicle Shyness
Grizzly Bear Tower Position
Ursus arctos horribilis

Sometimes you just want to be left alone, and usually a cubicle is a small enough space to ensure this. However, even cardboard walls can be breached, so you may have to take things a step further. An excellent start is the Grizzly Bear Tower Position. There are two elements to this method, and both are critically important. First, use only Intel-based computers to form the walls. Second, hand posture must be executed as shown. Follow these instructions and few workers will dare to invade your space.

Conference Inadequacy Syndrome
Northern Flying Squirrel Chair Posture
Glaucomys sabrinus

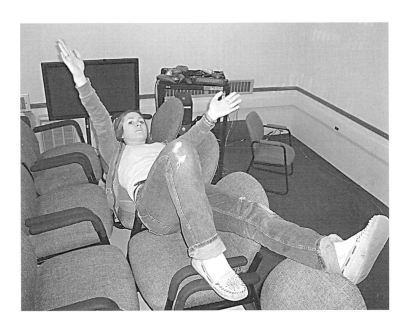

Having a seat at the table is important in the corporate world, but the highly competitive issue of conference room positioning is a foremost office stressor. This anxiety is caused by the fear that you will not have a chair of your own. To overcome this doubt, take ownership of all available conference room chairs. Place them on top of the conference room table, and place yourself on top of the chairs. Use your arms to indicate that these ALL belong to you. For best results put the chairs back before an actual meeting.

Loopism
Asiatic Clam Sea Posture
Corbicula fluminea

There is a fine line between inclusion and involvement. The Asiatic Clam teaches us to recognize this important distinction, and offers inspiration in a technique that keeps you on the chosen side of this perennial divide. As you assume a strong floor position, direct your gaze at the imagined surface of the powerful ocean above. From your vantage point on the sea floor you will achieve a clarity and singleness of purpose envied by others. The loop may be a trap, but this technique is a powerful defense.

Hyper Authoria
Wood Tick Covered Ear Stance
Dermacentor variabilis

You are a conscientious worker, but the daily barrage of orders, instructions, and commands threatens to overwhelm you. The problem is overly enthusiastic supervision, but since you don't have an actual office, you have no sanctuary. Your only recourse involves mobile reductionism. Place one hand over the ear closest to your boss. Use your other hand and one foot to counter the vestibular imbalance that can occur with this technique. You should immediately notice at least a fifty per cent improvement. Switch hands as needed.

Memo Deficiency
Bullfrog Ankle Flex Position
Rana catesbeiana

Effective memo writing is a skill that blends language, politics, foresight, and flexibility. The key is not to write the memo, but to visualize the memo after it is written. The Bullfrog calculates the trajectory of its next meal and then quickly acquires a tasty morsel. Likewise, you must anticipate thoughts before they emerge from your subconscious. With your ankle secured behind your neck, inhale, and focus your energy through your fingertips and into the keyboard. Now exhale as you become the memo.

Cubicle Fatigue
Northern Harrier Raised Arms Posture
Circus cyaneus

The inability to escape life in a cubicle is a shared office lament. While this does not in itself result in pathology, over many years the grind of life in a small gray space reduces energy. Take up a strong position in the dominant corner of your cube. The monitor is typically a focal point due to its glowing display, so take advantage of this. While in this position of control, symbolically revive your cubicle by vigorously raising your arms. Practice this technique every other day for six minutes to reinvigorate your work space.

Customer Symbiosis
Thompson Gazelle Extended Leg Stance
Gazella thomsoni

Sometimes your office duties are expanded, requiring you to engage in customer service. In such cases it is important to remain detached, as cubicle workers have a tendency to be overly generous, especially with returns or discounts. To dampen your natural empathy, try the Thompson Gazelle Extended Leg Stance. Symbolically distance yourself with a raised leg, and extend one arm as if to accept coworker support. If you practice this diligently your symbiosis should gradually diminish, but excessive use may cause cramping.

Interpersonal Communication Deficiency
Tricolored Blackbird Tail Flutter Movement
Agelaius tricolor

Some office workers find it difficult to connect with others. This important social skill can be improved, but it requires finesse and many hours of intense training. The Tricolored Blackbird socializes with other flock members by rapidly fluttering its tail feathers, teaching us the value of complex body language. Learn from this example. Reach back, back, as far as you can. Spread your fingers, and flutter for all you're worth. With your new-found confidence, soon they'll be calling you Mr. Communicator.

Anger Management Deficit
Northern Alligator Lizard Covered Hand Posture
Elgaria coerulea

Even the nicest people sometimes get angry, and in times of raging fury it can be difficult to maintain a pleasant demeanor. The Northern Alligator Lizard long ago learned that rage is no substitute for a positive attitude, and to this day will bask quietly in the sun, fuming, but in control. To achieve hegemony over your anger, follow his example. Find a convenient location, symbolically place your temper in your palm, and cover it with your other hand. Bask in the glory of your tranquility.

Socialization Illness
Northern Lobster Urgent Leg Stance
Homarus americanus

The difference between socializing and work-related schmoozing is not easy to detect. To the untrained eye, the two can be indistinguishable, but rest assured, management knows the difference. As a recognized disorder, Socialization Illness is eligible for reimbursement under Medicare part B, but only if accompanied by level four associative symptoms. Despite these limitations, prognosis for a full recovery is excellent. For best results hold this position for two minutes, twice a day, and avoid contact with others.

Your promptness is impeccable. In fact, you have never been late for a meeting, missed an appointment, or canceled an engagement. But this is not simply good manners—it is a treatable condition of timely excess. You must learn to overcome the feeling of guilt that accompanies the thought of lateness. Assume the above position to remind yourself that "time" has never really been understood by man. The goal of this technique is to position hands and feet in midair, symbolizing freedom from the constraint of schedules.

Java Management Deficiency
Pygmy Whitefish Teapot Stance
Certhia americana

Coffee-making is an art. You take a certain quantity of coffee, place it in the filter, and add water to the coffee machine. For best results the water should be fresh, cold, and untreated with chlorine or other additives. You then turn on the coffee machine. But most important, you must have the proper attitude. To achieve this requires a fine-tuned awareness of beverage nuance. If you find it difficult to achieve this level of discernment, the Pygmy Whitefish Teapot Stance can help. Just tilt, and pour.

Flexibility Strain
Rose Anemone Elevated Gumby Position
Tealia piscivora

Others like dealing with you because you're so easy to get along with. Unfortunately, headquarters prefers the hoop method of management, and insists that you be less flexible with coworkers. While you may have no choice but to implement this new way of doing business, take care not to lose your innate elasticity. Some day you may need it. To ensure that your supple attitude survives the latest management fad, regularly practice the Elevated Gumby Position. Your coworkers will be green with envy.

Office Agoraphobia
Scrub Jay Flying Desk Position
Aphelocoma californica

Sometimes you just want to get away, but you can't stand to leave your office. This inability to venture far from your work area is not only management's joy, but a debilitating condition. The Scrub Jay Flying Desk Position addresses this unfortunate dilemma with a unique blend of desk exercise and imagination. Assume a prone desktop position, spread your arms, and prepare for liftoff. You are cleared for a journey to anyplace you can envision. Just be sure to return by one o'clock.

Asking for time off shouldn't be cause for concern. After all, it's your vacation time, and you've earned a rest. Nevertheless, the days prior to submitting your leave request can cause serious stress. To inoculate yourself against anticipated drama, practice the Horned Puffin Skating Stance twice daily for a full week prior to asking for time off. This technique will not lessen management irritation, but it will put a smile on your face as you complete a triple and nail the landing. Be sure to smile as you pass the judges.

Font Compulsion
Painted Turtle Gaze Position
Chrysemys picta

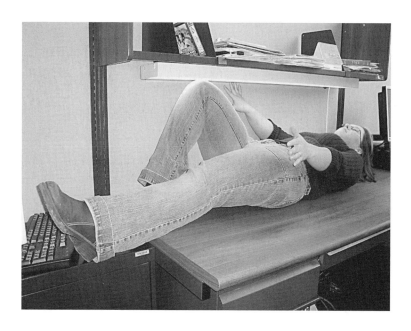

The urge to change the appearance of your text can be overpowering. Which typeset is best? If you frequently select a font, only to immediately switch to another, you may have Font Compulsion. This habitual need to modify has its roots in visual perfectionism, and can be treated, but the key is repetition. While staring into a florescent light, visualize a Frutiger Linotype. Hold for ten seconds. Now, without blinking, replace the Frutiger with a Garamond. Mentally repeat the cycle until you can no longer see a difference.

Hygienic Desk Compulsion
Spotted Bat Inversion Stance
Euderma maculatum

You cannot ignore buildup. As dust and other particulate matter accumulate on your desk it becomes increasingly difficult to accomplish even routine tasks—the debris is too distracting. For immediate relief, assume the Spotted Bat Inversion Stance, place a hygienic cloth between your head and the desk, and begin the cleansing process. From this vantage point you can see even the smallest particles, so the end result should be a desktop so clean you could eat off of it. But don't, because that would make a mess.

Compact Technology Deficiency
Red Abalone Drive Posture
Haliotus rufescens

A consistently jammed CD ROM tray is one of several symptoms of Compact Technology Deficiency. The key to avoiding such problems is preventative maintenance, in the form of the Red Abalone Drive Posture. This highly technical position enhances your drive proficiency, allowing you to sense disk-related problems before they occur. After practicing this technique it is not uncommon to sense disk failure from more distant workstations, but increased potassium has been shown to dampen this effect.

Chronic Email Delivery Failure
Common Porcupine Rising Heel Position
Erethizon dorsatum

If you suffer from chronic email delivery failure, the world can be a lonely place. To increase the likelihood of delivery, perform the Common Porcupine Rising Heel Position before pressing the send button. Scientists have no explanation for why this works, but it may be due to increased sensitivity in the peripheral nerve bundle. Be certain to elevate the heel no less than six inches above your waistline, with the left hand touching the ground throughout the elevation. Following execution, close and reopen your email program.

Music Download Fatigue
Coast Mole Cave Posture
Scapanus orarius

Music downloads are great for productivity, but waiting for free tune providers to deliver the goods can be exhausting. To prepare for your next grueling session, climb beneath your desk and assume the Coast Mole Cave Posture. Gently rest your head on your computer, and stretch your arm towards the nearest wireless access point. This will refresh your download vitality. When ready, emerge from your shelter and let the transfer begin. This technique works best with Hip Hop or Rap, but never use for seventies classics.

Overhappiness
Laughing Gull Twisted Spine Position
Larus atricilla

Too much happiness can be contagious, but before you start a pandemic of good humor, take a moment to think. Consider the plight of the Laughing Gull. Condemned to an existence filled with taunts and jeers, this noble flier compensates with an endless stream of unrequited chortles. To an outsider he appears happy, but in truth, he is over-happy. Remember, a man who laughs constantly has little time to work. The Twisted Spine Position will help you to moderate your bliss.

Insufficient Privilege Disorder
Bowhead Whale Raised Arm Stance
Balaena mysticetus

It is common in this world of ubiquitous technology to occasionally be denied access. However, if electronic rejection becomes habitual, the personal impact can be devastating. Learn to embrace that which denies you. To strengthen your acceptance in the automated world, assume a comfortable seated position and gently cradle an energized monitor. After a few minutes you should start to feel a strong mechanical bond. This is natural, but keep one arm free to maintain your humanity.

Thermal Uncertainty Disorder
Band-Tailed Pigeon Fan Stance
Columba fasciata

While your coworkers argue about the temperature settings, you are the one who suffers. One person sets the thermostat to sixty, and another bumps it up to eighty. Then the cycle repeats. You are left confused and cold. Or hot. Unfortunately, you live in a world of climactic chaos, you don't know what to do, and Thermal Uncertainty Disorder is the result. Your only recourse is the Band-Tailed Pigeon Fan Stance. Perhaps when your coworkers see how desperate you are they'll finally stop the madness.

Printer Envy
Northern Fur Seal Sheltering Arms Position
Callorhinus ursinus

You thought you had the best printer ever, but then you saw the four-color, eighty-page per minute beauty in the payroll office, and now you're not so sure. The department secretary has a totally awesome LaserJet, and even the dot matrix classic in the label making area is starting to look good. These are sure signs of Printer Envy. As with most electronic fixations, the best cure is to transfer your attention to something else. Assume a comfortable desk position and embrace your new friend. Oh my—that's a nice one.

Severe Control Sensitivity
Walnut Caterpillar Pressing Earth Posture
Datana ministra

There are many rules that we must follow without question, but some seem designed to simply impose control for control's sake. This can be literally maddening. If you feel like a pawn in the wacky world of corporate domination, then you may have developed Severe Control Sensitivity. While you can do little to impact arbitrary edicts from above, you can take charge of the universe beneath you. Put your full weight behind this effort at personal expression. Remember: in this office, you are the man.

Upgrade Paralysis
Penicillate Jellyfish Spinal Flex Position
Polyorchis penicillatus

It's not that you don't want to upgrade; you just have a low tolerance for pain. That's why you've been using the same operating system for seven years, and why your word processing software requires white-out to make changes. Your suspicion of so-called improvements actually puts you ahead of the curve, but it will not stop mandated progress. To help with the inevitable transition, try combining flexibility with technology. You should have time for several sets while the new operating system boots.

Chronic Expectation Disease
Starry Flounder Ceiling Position
Catostomus catostomus

Your optimism and positive outlook may keep your blood pressure down, but always expecting the best from others is risky. Unbridled exuberance takes a toll, and in extreme cases can develop into Chronic Expectation Disease. Symptoms typically include frequent smiling, bounciness, and glowing commentary. The Starry Flounder Ceiling Position reminds you that everyone has limits, and they are probably lower than yours. For best results maintain contact with the ceiling throughout this technique.

Web Inhibition
Washington Giant Earthworm Pivot Movement
Megascolides americanus

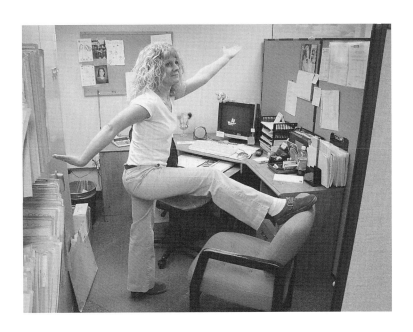

Almost everyone surfs the web during work hours. This is a well-known productivity tool. But to enjoy the full benefit of this common form of online therapy the viewer must relax. Sure, if your boss catches you making another stock buy it won't look so good, and that poker hand isn't going to cut it come review time. Nevertheless, you must learn to chill during online activities. The Washington Giant Earthworm Pivot Movement—which can be performed while browsing—is a powerful Internet guilt inhibitor.

Chronic Pragmatism
Virginia Opossum Oath Posture
Didelphis virginia

You never promise more than you can deliver, which leads to lowered expectations. This helps your reputation in the long run, but does little to secure important short term goals. To enhance the body's natural ability to over-commit, perform the Virginia Opossum Oath Posture twice daily. With one hand on a favorite book, raise your other hand and gently brush your toes across your desktop. Without making eye contact, offer a guarantee that the current project will be delivered on time. This posture helps balance realism.

Excessive Contribution Syndrome
Woodchuck Kneeling Posture
Marmota monax

The reason why everyone else has so much time to socialize is because you carry most of the work load. While this may appear to be an admirable trait, the others will someday be called to task for their mingling, and their careers will suffer. You are not helping by hoarding the work, and must learn to share it. From a kneeling position, with your right foot delicately touching your chair, vigorously reject twenty per cent of your current tasks. With regular practice you will eventually be satisfied with less.

Office Hygiene Compulsion
Northern Pintail Suspended Torso Stance
Anas acuta

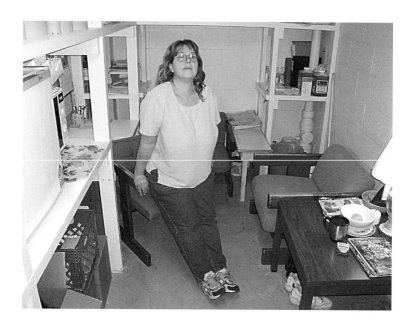

If you spend time at home thinking about how clean your work cubicle is, you almost certainly have Office Hygiene Compulsion. The Suspended Torso Stance will help you to overcome this need for purity in a very practical manner. Using a chair of suitable height and dimension, lift and hold your body as shown for as long as your arms can tolerate. Just when you feel your strength is about to fail, release. Repeat ten more times. When finished, your desire to clean your office should have diminished considerably.

Public Announcement Phobia
Black Throated Sparrow Screaming Knee Stance
Eubalaena glacialis

Public speaking is one of the highest ranked fears, topped only by fear of public singing, and dancing. For you, the thought of using the office intercom system is cause for the deepest dread. Relax. The Black Throated Sparrow Screeming Knee Stance is a boisterous posture that incorporates well-founded psychological principles with a natural approach to healing. Hold the knee close to horizontal while exhaling sharply. Periodically rotate the thumbs. With practice, you will soon begin to anticipate work broadcasts with joy.

Illumination Catatonia
Northern Bobwhite Hovering Moonbeam Position
Colinus virginianus

Simply put, light immobilizes you. The brighter it is, the slower you become. On those rare occasions when they replace the florescent bulbs, you are positively inert. This is a common ailment among long-term office workers, who are used to spending much of their time in the dark. The cure is curiously simple: more of what bothers you. To acclimate yourself, position a chair as close to a bright light as is practical. To avoid attracting unwanted attention use a standard office work chair, and look nonchalant.

Belted Kingfisher Hovering Stride Position
Ceryle alcyon

This is the generation of homeland security. As Tom Ridge, former Director of Homeland Security, and Erie, Pennsylvania native so eloquently might have stated: "It's important to lock the doors." This helps us to remember the necessity of an integrated security system, preferably incorporating triple redundancy and level three outer perimeter countermeasures. In lieu of this, perform the Belted Kingfisher Hovering Stride Position. Remain aloft for three seconds while firmly touching a nearby grid pattern.

Automation Dependency
Gray Catbird Robot Position
Dumetella carolinensis

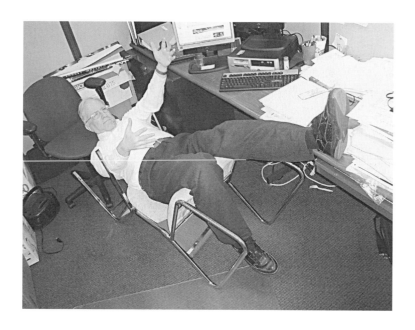

Computers are here to stay. This has made life much easier in some regards, but reliance on technology can cause other skills to atrophy. Virtually every technique that combats Automation Dependency involves replication therapy. In this case, use the Gray Catbird Robot Position to become the technology. Allow your mentality to be consumed by pure logic, as you rigidly move your joints in robotic precision. After a few minutes you should begin to think in binary terms. This is a sure sign that the healing process has begun.

Email Sensitivity Dysfunction
Western Harvest Mouse Extended Nose Posture
Reithrodontomys megalotis

Sometimes it's difficult to sense when important email has arrived without opening your inbox. Sadly, when humans migrate into cubicles they often lose the ability to smell new messages. To recover this sense, employ the Western Harvest Mouse Extended Nose Posture. Start very close, and try to get a whiff of the most recent email. This will be the freshest message, and easiest to detect. Don't worry about content at first. As your nasal sensitivity increases, accuracy will improve. Do not try this with instant messages.

Scribe's Anarchy
Purple Finch Tilted Hip Position
Carpodacus purpureus

With a drawer full of pens, it can be a daunting task to select the right one for a particular task. Some simply grasp the nearest Bic, but this haphazard approach to writing can only lead to trouble. If you are going to spend time doing a job, spend time selecting the right tool. The Purple Finch Tilted Hip Position is the ideal technique for pondering this ancient dilemma. With one hand make the shape of paper, and with the other, a rock. Now tilt. If you do not instantly know which pen to use, tilt the other way.

Humor Fundamentalism
Sea Cucumber Shelf Position
Parastichopus californicus

When those in a position of power are also moderately funny people, there is a tendency to codify humorous interplay. This radicalization of hilarity typically limits would-be comics to authorized subject matter, as documented in carefully guarded manuals. The end result is to actually stifle funniness, but in its early stages Humor Fundamentalism is very treatable. The Sea Cucumber Shelf Position is known as a somber balm, and the extended arm protocol provides a particularly effective liberal counterbalance.

Cubicle Inadequacy
Northern River Otter Elevated Head Position
Lontra canadensis

In nature, height equals superiority. This principle can easily be extended into the office, but unfortunately most office chairs are very limited in their scalability. Thus, achieving demonstrable altitude dominance presents a challenge. The Northern River Otter Elevated Head Position offers a solution to this conundrum, but it requires a prepared platform for successful execution. Gather several chairs and stack them to the desired height. Ascend. This confidence-building position requires several applications for full effect.

Office Sedentary Disorder
San Francisco Brine Shrimp Gleeful Leg Stance
Artemia franciscana

Hour after hour of sitting in front of a computer takes a serious toll on your body. Much like astronauts in a weightless environment, your body responds by losing both muscle tone and flexibility. Worse, your mind is not far behind. It is critical to your survival to counter this atrophy with aggressive neuromuscular therapy. Using a desk for foot support, stand erect and perform a one-handed wave. Close one eye, and mentally release accumulated melancholy. Perform at least twice weekly.

Equipment Infatuation
European Rabbit Hug Position
Oryctolagus cuniculus

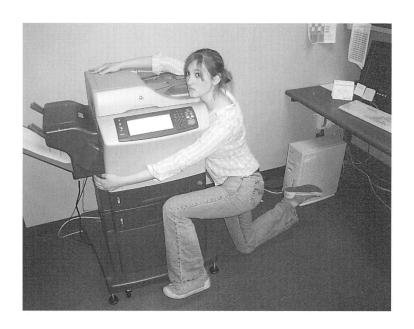

Office workers spend a lot of time with copiers, shredders, printers, and other workplace devices. It is natural that a bond will sometimes form with a special piece of equipment, but it is important to maintain professional distance. A casual embrace is symbolic of platonic friendship, and is also the method of choice in the European Rabbit Hug Position. With your right foot elevated, assure your favorite machine that you will always be good friends. To reduce potential awkwardness, be prepared with a joke or anecdote.

Menu Dyslexia
Snapping Turtle Eastern Breeze Position
Chelydra serpentine

Menu flow is critical to application navigation, but it seems that every software package has its own way of getting from point to point. Some workers naturally assimilate new menus, while others are less adept. For you it is chaos. You are not alone. Experts estimate that millions suffer from Menu Dyslexia, and sadly, most go untreated. For temporary relief, take a seated position, and point both arms and a leg towards the menu Help button. Exhale. Point. Click. Inhale. Repeat every ten minutes while running a new application.

Cubicle Claustrophobia
Evening Grosbeak Cube Position
Coccothraustes vespertinus

New office workers waste a lot of time trying to adjust to the small space available in most cubicles. Americans have grown up with a super-size mentality, and the super-small square footage they are assigned for eight hours a day can cause Cubicle Claustrophobia. To prevent this, many employers now use a cube trainer. Any employee who spends a couple weeks in the trainer will be delighted with their allotted workspace. The Evening Grosbeak Cube Position is the standard technique used with this device.

Chair Aversion
Mosquito Fish Floor Posture
Gambusia affinis

If you work in an office for a living, Chair Aversion is a serious condition. Equipment such as keyboards and telephones are usually positioned for use from a seated position, and while it is possible to operate such devices while standing, efficiency will suffer. The best course is to cure the disease. The Mosquito Fish Floor Posture is designed to help you understand the chair's perspective, and thereby gain insight into your own misgivings. Hold for one minute. Then see how many times you can spin around.

Office Nomadism
Northern Elephant Seal Horizontal Posture
Mirounga angustirostris

The urge to wander to distant places may simply be a hereditary trait, but it is not welcome in the workplace. To be sure, you understand that management expects you to spend most of your time at your desk, but the lure of far off cubicles is irresistible. It's not that you want to walk aimlessly from cube to cube, chatting with anyone who will give you the time of day. It just…happens. The Northern Elephant Seal Horizontal Posture may be the answer to your woes. Simply secure yourself as shown.

Office Myopia
Common Raccoon Focal Position
Procyon lotor

It is possible to become so attuned to the details of your own task that you lose site of the larger goal. In fact, this is an important aspect of planned knowledge deficit, a common strategy for managing teams of workers. The key is focus. Learn to concentrate only on the job at hand, disregarding any and all distractions. With your thumb and forefinger, block your peripheral vision with an impenetrable seal of flesh. Place a cookie or other desert item on your extended leg. When you can resist this tasty morsel, you are ready.

Quadrangular Stress
Moon Snail Upward Gaze Position
Poilnices lewisii

Because of their geometric compatibility, cubicles are a highly sought-after work space, but not everyone is blessed with four cardboard walls. This can lead to Quadrangular Stress. Square dancing is the basis for many types of therapy, and now the natural evolution of this increasingly popular relaxation technique has brought it into the modern office. Select a suitably shaped chair, sashay onto the main platform, and promenade your tension away. For a more intense workout, consider a brisk dosado.

Acquired Window Deficiency
Side-blotched Lizard Float Position
Uta stansburiana

The office with the coveted window usually becomes available only with the retirement or death of a coworker, so being denied this treasured piece of real estate can be a traumatic experience. The only way to overcome this paralyzing distress is through levitation, which requires both mental focus and physical control. Concentrate your gaze, lift both arms, and rise, rise! Hover for ten seconds, and then relax. As you slowly drift earthward release your anguish. Repeat as needed.

Noonism
Foolish Mussel Chop-Five Position
Mytilus trossulus

The wistful longing for noon is symptomatic of other underlying conditions, and can include almost any of the maladies described in this book. To address this secondary disorder, a simultaneous monitor chop and high five posture is sometimes effective, but only when performed from a seated position in conjunction with a raised foot position. This is a complex treatment regimen that only yields results when practiced regularly. Some therapists have reported positive outcomes when combined with snacks.

Notification Disorder
Ribbon Worm Desk Stance
Tubulanus annulatus

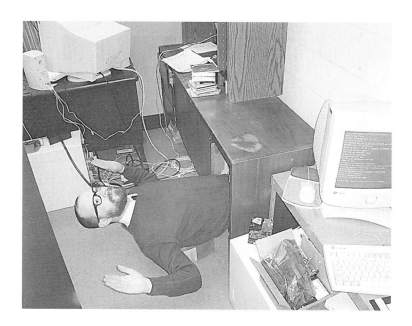

If you have difficulty calling in sick, the solution is obvious: planning. Assume the Ribbon Worm Desk Stance two days prior to your anticipated illness. Hold until management notices. If you are not immediately asked to take some time off, this meditative posture should at least provide some credibility for that upcoming phone call. The communication skills that you gain from this technique may carry over into other problem areas, such as dealing with telemarketers. Do not use if taking laxatives.

Perch Empathy
Gray Wolf Squatting Posture
Canis lupus

Isolation in a cubicle or office for endless hours, days, weeks, or even years may eventually lead you to regard inanimate objects as close friends. A specific case of this is Perch Empathy, an unusual fondness for a chair, stool, or other sitting device. This syndrome is characterized by extreme guilt for perceived abuse. To overcome this malady, assume the Gray Wolf Squatting Posture, talk nicely to the object, gently massage its arms, and reassure it that it is a valued item. Follow with a cup of herbal tea.

Group Dynamics Deficiency
Giant Rock Scallop Horizontal March Stance
Crassadoma gigantean

It's fine to march to the beat of a different drummer, but sometimes it is necessary to work together as a group. While your staunch individualism is a leadership asset, for those times when you are needed as a simple cog it can be a hindrance. To induce the appropriate blend of relaxation and rigid conformity, try the Giant Rock Scallop Horizontal March Stance. Maintain an eyes-front posture as you execute a lock-step leg pose. After mastering the horizontal position, try the standing version for enhanced compliance.

Complacency Syndrome
Pacific White-Sided Dolphin Arm Stance
Lagenorhynchus obliquidens

Remaining on task is a good thing; remaining on the same task for five years is not. The boredom associated with working on the same project for an extended period of time is a leading cause of Complacency Syndrome. A unique approach to this long-term problem combines revivalism with physical exertion. It has long been understood that a mind-body connection exists, and can be accessed. When performing this technique, ascend the highest platform available. Extend your arms. Rejoice, and be refreshed.

Cosmos Perception Disorder
Ord's Kangaroo Rat Squeeze Posture
Dipodomys ordii

Sometimes it seems as though the universe consists only of your workplace, which can be overwhelming. The boundless crush of the seemingly infinite corporate colossus can overpower the frailty of those enveloped by its grandeur. If you have Cosmos Perception Disorder, you understand this all too well. While the problem here is one of perception, the feelings are quite real. For peace of mind, find the smallest space that will accommodate your frame, and squeeze into it. You may have to hold your breath, but the relief is worth it.

Scrounger's Anemia
Dungeness Crab Crawl Position
Cancer magister

Your refusal to discard virtually any office supply is a virtuous example of frugality, but you should remember that there are limits to thrift. Trying to exact the last ounce of toner, the final bit of whiteout, or even the ultimate crumb of eraser off the nub of pencil that you have so carefully nursed for all these years, can render you impotent. To restore balance, practice the Dungeness Crab Crawl Position. The optional raised palm is a symbol of economic surrender, and indicates a readiness to splurge.

Assistive Disorder
Olympia Oyster Holding Boulder Position
Ostrea conchaphila

A cooperative spirit indicates a gracious character, but excessive helpfulness can be a personal detriment when practiced without proper training. Don't be overwhelmed; be prepared. The Olympia Oyster Holding Boulder Position reconciles the weight of demand with the need for balance. Perform this crucial facilitative technique early in the morning. Use your left hand to suspend a symbolic boulder of responsibility ominously above you. Your other hand provides stability. For a finer adjustment use your foot.

Task Exuberance
River Crayfish Stride Position
Orconectus virilis

Excitement over a work assignment is uplifting, but excessive thrill of duty can be harmful. As with many such conditions, finding equilibrium is the key. To lower dangerously high enthusiasm levels, and to reduce work adrenalin, a brisk power walk around your desk is the best remedy. A zesty romp near the window may help moderate your spirits further, but be careful not to overdo it. Most workers can tolerate no more than three complete laps. Remember to maintain proper arm posture throughout.

Acute Indifference
Beach-Dune Tiger Beetle Ridge Position
Cicindela hirticollis

The irony of indifference is that once you have it, you lose all interest in getting rid of it. One of the few techniques that can help is the Beach-Dune Tiger Beetle Ridge Position. As you feel interest wane, scale your work area and assume a prone position near the sharp edge of the desktop. Lift your feet, and extend one arm into space. Try to fully employ this position before the zenith of your malaise. The excruciating pain that you will endure is no picnic, but it should easily take the place of your disinterest.

Low Work Esteem
Monarch Butterfly Man of Steel Stance
Danaus plexippus

If you go through life thinking that everyone else's work is better than yours, you may have Low Work Esteem. Although your assessment is probably not entirely correct, why take chances? The solution to this problem is a heavy dose of overcompensation. You must convince yourself that your work product is the result of a superior skill set, that your ability is superhuman. The Man of Steel Stance reinforces this fanciful notion, but be advised that severe cases may require a cape.

Task Resistance
Striped Scorpion Toe Stance
Centruroides vittatus

Work tasks often take on almost human characteristics, and will resist you until the bitter end. The natural reaction is to push back, which only leads to frustration. Avoid direct clashes. An oblique assault on the offending assignment is the suggested approach. The Striped Scorpion Toe Stance improves your ability to employ peripheral tactics, and the key is to remain as still as possible in a concealed flanking position. Maintain toe discipline, and keep hands combat-ready throughout. Your task will never know what hit it.

Identity Paranoia
Walnut Caterpillar Mask Posture
Datana ministra

The electronic universe is filled with rogues who would assume your identity for evil purposes. Every time you turn on your computer, legions of spies probe your defenses for vulnerabilities, seeking to exploit any opening. Every phone call, email, or whispered conversation is an opportunity for them to usurp your persona for vile gain. They are everywhere, and now you have Identity Paranoia. To protect yourself, before booting up, cover up. This posture is not merely symbolic; organic masking may even reduce spam.

Monitor Pox
Bald Eagle Cabinet Stance
Haliaeetus leucocephalus

Caused by a virus, Monitor Pox is characterized by small, bumpy pixilation, and can cause irritation in end users. The incubation period for this disorder is 7 to 21 days after exposure, but flat screens may progress more quickly. For relief from symptoms, calamine lotion can be applied, but this may make it difficult to use the display. Older monitors are more at risk for severe symptoms. The most effective approach involves distance, so stand up, step back, and stay away. The Cabinet Stance helps maintain a proper interval.

File Phobia
Masai Giraffe One Foot Chair Stance
Giraffa camelopardalis

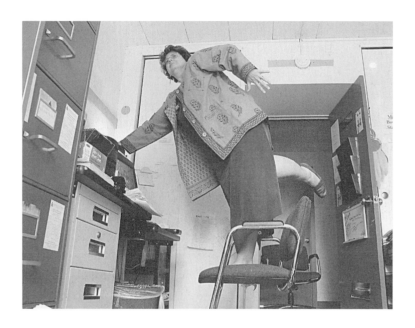

Your filing system has been declared a disorganized crime, and just the thought of trying to find something gives you cold sweats. Perhaps the shredder would have been a better long-term solution, but it is far too late for that. Now you have File Phobia. Before diving in, prep yourself with this two-step program. From an elevated position flex your elbow, and follow with a vigorous rearward kick. A sea of manila is the last place you want to spend your day, but this technique may lessen your anxiety.

Office Vertigo
Lake Chub Hanging Cloud Stance
Couesius plumbeus

While inexplicable company guidelines are generally the product of dedicated committees, they can still give you vertigo, draining the blood from your head with mind-numbing quickness. You know it's coming, so now is the time to prepare. As soon as any committee of company elders convenes, immediately assume the Lake Chub Hanging Cloud Stance. The pooling of blood in your head will compensate for office policies so baffling they'll make your head spin. For annual reports, double the dose.

In the office it is important to remain calm, cool, and collected, but sometimes workplace news is so stunning you cannot suppress a reaction. This reflexive display of emotion could cost you that next promotion, so don't let it happen. Be proactive. Preemptively startle in the privacy of your cubicle before the news happens. When the dramatic story arrives, you will already have reacted. Your dependably stoic response will become the stuff of legend, as even upper management seeks your measured counsel. Use twice daily.

Inbox Aversion
Longfin Smelt Desk Cartwheel
Spirinchus thaleichthys

Once you see the email subject line, you have lost plausible deniability. To truthfully disavow knowledge, you must never see the message arrive. The key is to carefully monitor the Outlook refresh indicator, and take action before your inbox is updated. There is little time for your typical, measured egress. Instead, as soon as that icon starts flashing, launch the desk cartwheel and get out of there. This technique should be reserved for emergency situations, such as Help Desk requests, or just before lunch.

Challenge Deficiency
Coho Salmon Chair Dive Position
Oncorhynchus kisutch

When scuba divers become bored with routine visits to offshore wrecks or coral reefs, they sometimes turn to more titillating activities, such as cave diving. The exploration of underwater caves requires specialized training, and can be quite dangerous. Similarly, some office workers are not sufficiently challenged by their daily routine, and require a more exciting diversion. The Chair Dive is an exhilarating position that blends the perilous elements of cave diving with office furniture. Use redundant lighting for safety.

Partitionism
Box Crab Barricade Stance
Calappa ocellata

Inexplicable fondness for a cubicle wall may seem like a harmless affliction, but this weakness for fabric-covered cardboard can be a serious impediment. The problem arises when someone else is infatuated with *your* wall. It is impossible to concentrate on work while someone is making partition overtures in your workspace, so when the wall suitor approaches—they can often be identified by excessive perfume or cologne—immediately lay claim to the favored divide. Be prepared for a fight, as these things can turn ugly.

Nosebleeds
Northwestern Crow Pulling Earth Position
Corvus caurinus

Picture yourself here in
your favorite position.

X

If you have practiced the techniques described here with even minimal diligence, then you have almost certainly experienced nosebleeds. While this can be alarming, you are to be congratulated. The first step in achieving office wellness sometimes involves overt signs of physical distress. This is because your body and mind have grown weak from a sedentary lifestyle, but your fluids are now responding to a dynamic change in daily regimen. Good job! Reward yourself with three minutes in the Northwestern Crow Pulling Earth Position, then start again from page one.

Afterthoughts

This book started as a wisp of an idea, was propelled by the momentum of humor, and culminated in the previous series of photographs and exposition. Along the way over one hundred humans joined me in an adventure that will end in a few short pages.

I hope that you have enjoyed reading this manual as much as I enjoyed writing it. If you look through the book again, you will notice that nearly every model has a serious expression on their face. This was by design, but was almost always preceded and followed by a certain amount of giggling.

Ironically, in a majority of cases the models actually complained that their muscles were strained as they tried to perform the requested stance or position. For a spoof the book apparently did a pretty good job of toning. For the record, all poses were shot as you see them. The only editing was for shadowing or general picture quality.

If you enjoyed the book, please tell others. A book lives or dies by word of mouth, so please tell everyone about The Official Guide to Office Wellness. If your organization is planning an employee event, contact Bayla Publishing at the website below to arrange a booksigning or author presentation.

Final advice: Find your passion and indulge it. Life is short.

www.baylapublishing.com

Index of Maladies

Malady | Page

Malady	Page

Malady	Page

BAYLA
PUBLISHING

www.baylapublishing.com